February
Patterns & Projects

Newbridge Educational Publishing, LLC
New York

The purchase of this book entitles the buyer to duplicate
these pages for use by students in the buyer's classroom.
All other permissions must be obtained from the publisher.

© 2000 Newbridge Educational Publishing, LLC,
333 East 38th Street, New York, NY 10016. All rights reserved.

ISBN: 1-58273-130-6

Photo Credit: (cover and title page) Philip Bailey/The Stock Market

Table of Contents

Learning About Groundhogs 5
Wake Up, Groundhog! File-Folder Game. 6
The Wake-Up Song 11
Groundhog Paper-Bag Puppet 12
Groundhog Day Puppet Show 16

Valentine's Day Cards 17
Valentine Envelope 21
Valentine Zoo 22
Valentine Mailbag 24

Class Cupids 25
Mouse Beanbag 25
Beanbag Toss 28
"Cupid Says" Game 28
Valentine's Day Lotto Game 29

President's Day Class Discussion 33
President's Day Mobile 34
Legends of the Presidents 38
President's Day Bulletin Board 39
Washington's Three-Cornered Hat 43
Lincoln's Stovepipe Hat 44

Friendship Song 45
Fables of Friendship Flannel Board 46
Fables of Friendship Flannel Board Stories 50
The Lion and the Mouse 50
The Ant and the Dove 51
Aesop's Fables Class Discussion 52
Dramatize the Fables 52
Animal Families 53
Friendship Day Recommended Reading 54

Healthy Teeth File-Folder Game 55
Healthy Teeth Posters 60
Teeth Collages 60
Healthy Teeth Mobile 61
Happy Tooth, Sad Tooth Book 65
Lose-a-Tooth Experience Chart 66

Table of Contents (Continued)

Famous African-Americans Bulletin Board **67**
Jackie Robinson 68
Thurgood Marshall 70
Marian Anderson 72
George Washington Carver 74
Plant a Peanut 76
Peanut Butter 76
Martin Luther King, Jr. 77
Harriet Tubman 79

LEARNING ABOUT GROUNDHOGS

Share with children the following information about groundhogs. Then follow up with the activities on pages 6 through 16.

What animal helps us predict the weather? It's the groundhog! Every year on February 2, people watch the groundhog to see what it will do. February 2 is known as Groundhog Day. You might also call it Woodchuck Day, because *wood-chuck* is another name for groundhog. According to stories that have been passed down through the years, February 2 is the day the groundhog wakes up from its long winter sleep. The animal sticks its head out of its underground home and looks around. If the sun is shining and the groundhog sees its shadow, the animal is frightened and crawls back into its hole. People think that means there will be six more weeks of winter weather. But if it is a cloudy day and the groundhog does not see its shadow, the animal stays outside. People believe this means that spring weather will come soon.

Groundhogs live in parts of the United States and in Canada. The average groundhog is about two feet long (about the size of a small puppy), including its bushy tail. A groundhog looks very similar to a squirrel, except it's much larger. It has a flat head and its body is covered with a tough fur. The fur is gray on the upper parts of the body and yellowish-orange on the lower parts.

Groundhogs live in underground homes called burrows. They dig several different tunnels, so their homes have many rooms. To make their home, groundhogs first dig the burrows with the sharp claws of their front feet. Then they scrape the dirt out of the hole with their hind feet.

Groundhogs like to eat plants such as alfalfa and clover. These foods may please them, but it doesn't make the farmers happy! Farmers think groundhogs are pests because they eat their crops.

In the fall, groundhogs eat lots and lots of food. Then they crawl into their burrows and hibernate, or sleep through the winter, just like bears. The extra food they eat turns to fat in their bodies. Groundhogs live on the fat while they are sleeping. Then, on February 2, some groundhogs happen to be awakened from their slumber by a bright light or loud noise and come outside again. Another Groundhog Day!

WAKE UP, GROUNDHOG! FILE-FOLDER GAME

HOW TO MAKE

You need:
- crayons or markers
- scissors
- glue
- letter-sized file folder
- oaktag
- brass fastener
- clear contact paper
- envelope

1. Reproduce the game board, spinner, arrow, and playing pieces on pages 8 through 10 once. Have children color everything except the playing pieces and cut out.
2. Mount the game board on the inside of a letter-sized file folder.
3. Mount the spinner and arrow on oaktag. Poke a brass paper fastener through the middle of the arrow and spinner.
4. Color each of the playing pieces a different color. Mount on oaktag, laminate, and cut out.
5. Reproduce the "How to Play" instructions on page 7. Color, cut out, and mount on the front of the file folder.
6. Glue an envelope to the back of the folder to store the playing pieces.

WAKE UP, GROUNDHOG! FILE-FOLDER GAME

HOW TO PLAY
(for 2 to 3 players)

1. Each child chooses a playing piece and places it at the bottom of a groundhog's tunnel.
2. The youngest player goes first, and play proceeds clockwise around the board.
3. The first player spins and moves his or her playing piece the number of spaces indicated on the spinner. If "lose a turn" is spun, that player loses his or her next turn. If "spin again" is spun, that player may move one space and then spin again. (Only one "spin again" is allowed during each turn.)
4. If a player lands on a "+1" space, he or she moves ahead one space. If a player lands on a "-1" space, he or she moves back one space.
5. The first player to reach the top of his or her tunnel is the winner.

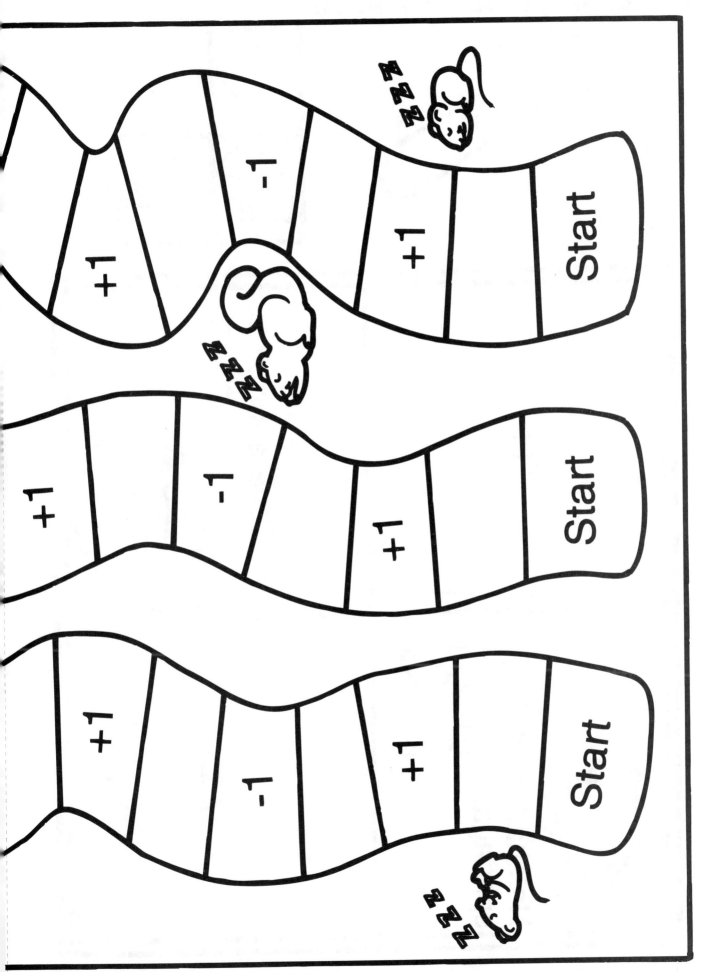

Start

Start

Start

9

1

Lose a turn.

No shadow, spin again.

2

THE WAKE-UP SONG
(sung to the tune of "Twinkle, Twinkle, Little Star")

Teach children the following song on Groundhog Day. Ask each child to curl up in a ball and pretend to be hibernating. As they sing the song, have children slowly uncurl and stand up, then stretch, rub their stomachs, and look all around.

Wake up, Groundhog,
Time to see
What the weather's
Going to be.
Time to stretch,
Time to think,
Time to eat,
And time to drink.
Wake up, Groundhog,
Time to see
What the weather's
Going to be!

GROUNDHOG PAPER-BAG PUPPET

You need:
• crayons or markers
• scissors
• glue
• medium-sized brown paper bags (one for each child)
• buttons, sequins, yarn

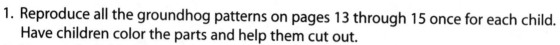

1. Reproduce all the groundhog patterns on pages 13 through 15 once for each child. Have children color the parts and help them cut out.
2. Have each child glue the groundhog head to the bottom of a medium-sized brown paper bag, as shown.
3. Ask each child to glue the groundhog body and legs to the front of the bag, as shown.
4. Help each child fold down the groundhog tail on the dotted line. Then have them glue the tail to the back of the bag, as shown.
5. Allow each child to personalize his or her puppet by adding buttons, sequins, yarn, and other available decorating materials.

Step 2

Step 3

Step 4

Groundhog Head Pattern

Groundhog Body Pattern

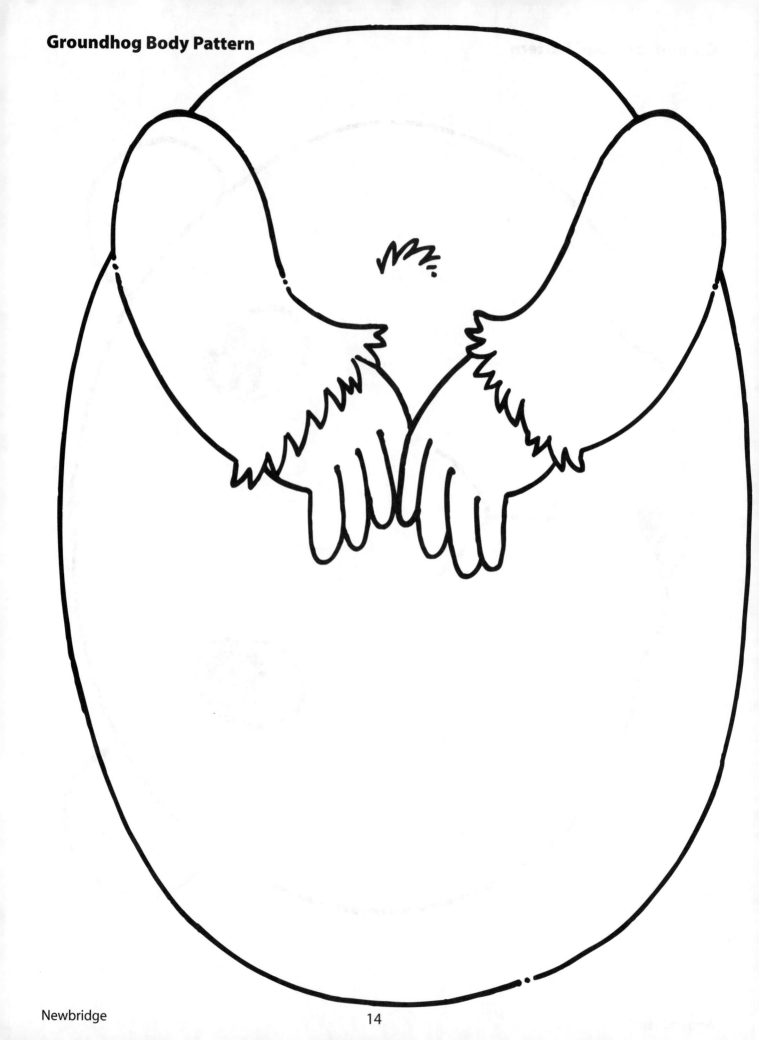

Groundhog Legs and Tail Patterns

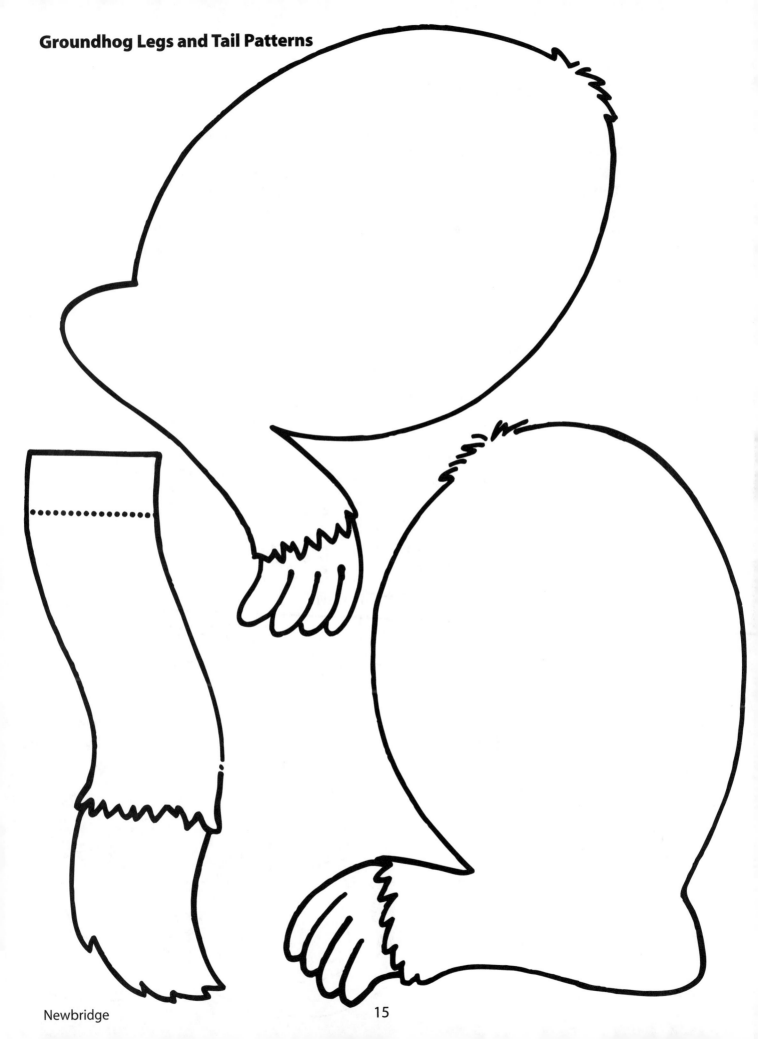

GROUNDHOG DAY PUPPET SHOW

1. Make a puppet stage by cutting a rectangle from one side of a large appliance box, as shown. Or, simply turn a classroom table over on its side.
2. If desired, have children make scenery for the puppet stage using construction paper, crayons or markers, glitter, cotton balls, and other available materials. Or, simply make a large sun and a few clouds that children can use in their dramatizations.
3. Choose volunteers to use their puppets to portray groundhogs emerging from their holes and reacting to the weather conditions. Let children make up their own dialogue.
4. As a group activity, teach children this poem to say while manipulating their groundhog puppets:

Little groundhog, little groundhog, how do you know
If it will be sunny, or if it will snow?
If pleasant warm breezes or cold winds will blow?
On February Second, your shadow tells us so!

VALENTINE'S DAY CARDS

You need:
- index cards
- grocery bag
- crayons or markers
- scissors
- glitter, ribbon, tissue paper

1. Write each child's name on an index card. Place the index cards in a grocery bag and let each child choose one card. Each child will make a valentine for the person whose name is on the card he or she has chosen.
2. Let each child choose a card pattern on pages 18 through 20. Reproduce the selected card once for each child.
3. Have children color and cut out the cards.
4. Help children fold the cards on the dotted lines, as shown.
5. Encourage children to decorate their cards with glitter, ribbon, tissue paper, and other available materials.
6. Ask children to write the names of their valentines on the cards. Then have children write or dictate messages on the inside of their cards.

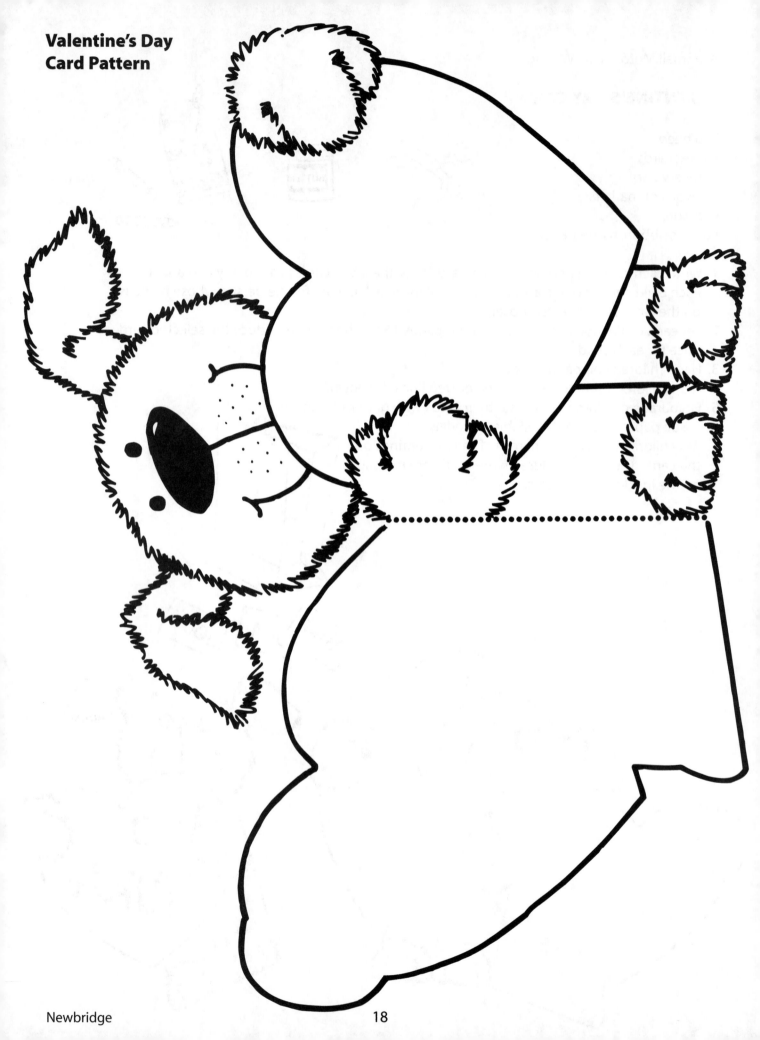

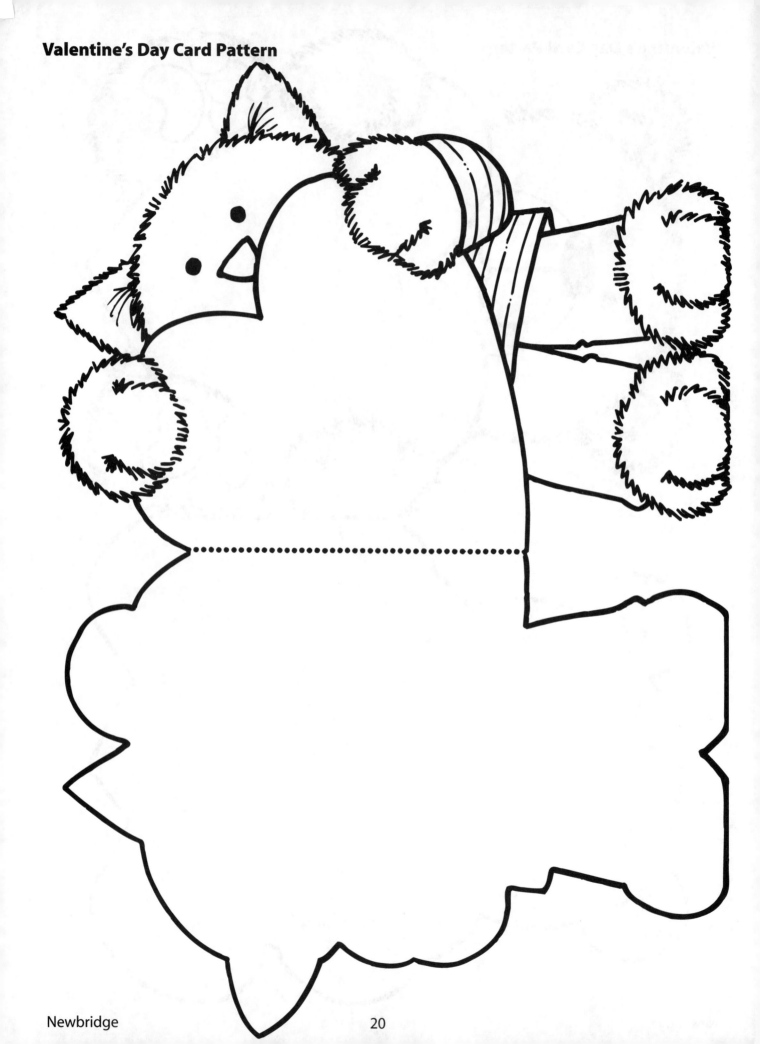

VALENTINE ENVELOPE

1. Reproduce the seals below once for each child. Have children color the seals and cut out.
2. Give each child a 9" x 12" piece of construction paper. Tell children to fold the paper, as shown, leaving 1" at the top.
3. Glue the sides of the envelopes together.
4. Help each child fold down the top flap. Tell each child to glue a seal over the flap, as shown, after placing a card inside.
5. Ask each child to write the name of the person to whom he or she is giving the valentine on the front of each envelope. Children may also use the seals as "stamps" for their envelopes.

Step 4

Step 2

HOWDY!

HI !

HELLO!

HI !

HOWDY!

Art/Small Motor Skills/Writing/Storytelling

VALENTINE ZOO

You need:
- scissors
- oaktag
- different types and colors of paper (construction paper, newsprint, oaktag, tissue paper, wrapping paper, and so on)
- glue
- crayons or markers
- pushpins or tacks

1. Reproduce the concentric hearts pattern on page 23 five times. Cut out so you have five hearts of different sizes. Trace each heart onto oaktag and cut out.
2. Have children trace around the oaktag patterns on different types of paper, creating hearts of all colors, textures, and sizes. Help children cut out the hearts.
3. Give a handful of hearts to each child. Ask children to experiment with the different sizes and shapes to create heart animals, as shown.
4. Have children mount their heart animals on construction paper and color. Encourage children to draw background scenery.
5. Children may write or dictate stories about their invented animals: where they live, their names, the types of foods they eat, and so on.
6. Collect the finished pictures and attach them to a wall or bulletin board. Title the display "Valentine Zoo."

Concentric Hearts Pattern

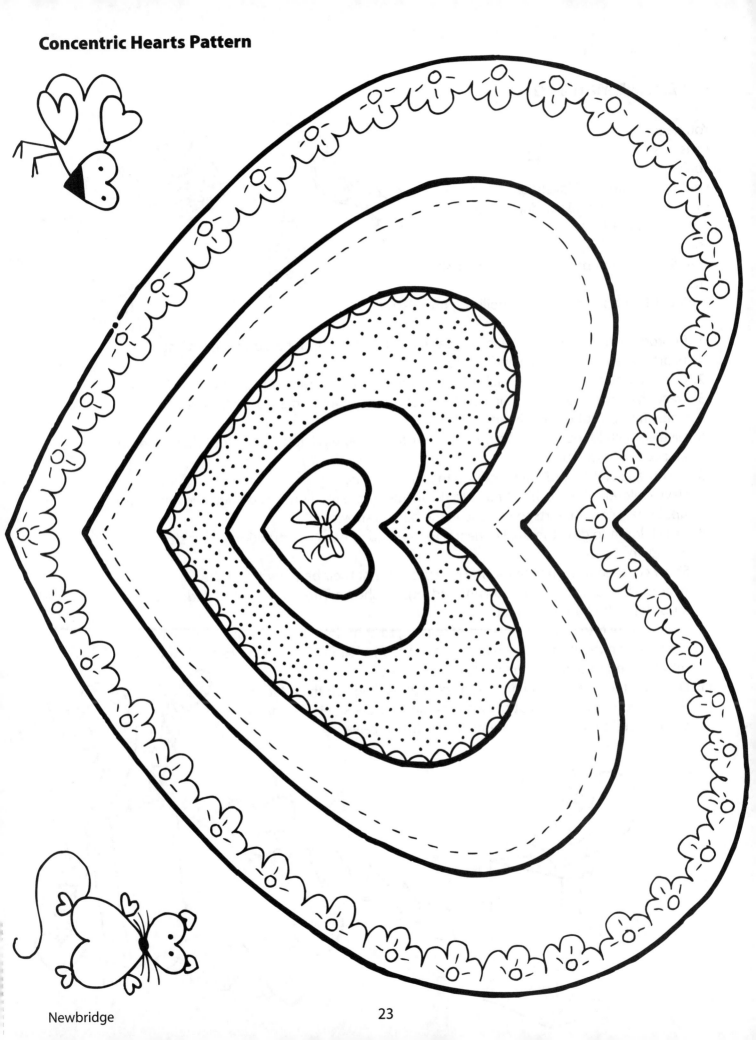

VALENTINE MAILBAG

You need:
- scissors
- oaktag
- red, pink, white, and lavender construction paper
- 1" x 10" strips of construction paper
- crayons or markers
- glue
- medium-sized paper bags (white, if possible)
- tape

Optional: fabric scraps, foil, lace, doilies, glitter, yarn

1. Reproduce the concentric hearts on page 23 once and cut out around the largest heart. Trace it onto oaktag and cut out.
2. Cut out around one of the smaller hearts. Trace it onto oaktag and cut out.
3. Trace the large heart onto colored construction paper four times for each child.
4. Help children cut out the hearts.
5. Give each child four 1" x 10" strips of construction paper. Help children fold their strips in an accordion manner.
6. Encourage children to draw faces on the large hearts.
7. Have children glue the heart faces to the inside of the medium-sized bags, allowing the upper part of the hearts to rise above the bag, as shown.
8. Ask children to glue the smaller hearts to one end of each construction paper strip, as shown.
9. Show children how to tape the strips to the sides of their bags, two near the top and two near the bottom, thus forming arms and legs, as shown. The hearts on the ends of the strips form the hands and feet.
10. Ask each child to decorate the rest of the bag to complete the body, and to write his or her name on the front of the bag. (If desired, fabric, foil, lace, doilies, glitter, and/or yarn may be used to decorate the mailbag.)
11. On Valentine's Day, ask children to place the mailbags on the edges of their desks or tables so that the legs dangle over the sides. The mailbags can be used to hold all the valentines children receive.

Step 7

Step 9

CLASS CUPIDS

You need:
• crayons or markers
• scissors
• hole puncher
• string or yarn
Optional: glue, oaktag

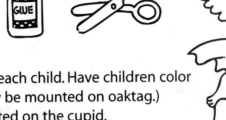

1. Reproduce one cupid pattern on page 26 for each child. Have children color the cupids and cut out. (If desired, cupids may be mounted on oaktag.)
2. Have children write their names where indicated on the cupid.
3. Punch a hole near the top of each cupid's head and tie a long length of string or yarn to it. Attach the strings to the ceiling in one corner of the room.
4. Explain to children that Valentine's Day is a special time to celebrate friendship, and that cupids are symbols of Valentine's Day.
5. The week before Valentine's Day, focus on consideration for others and friendship using the cupids hanging from the ceiling. Put stars on the wings of each cupid to represent acts of friendship among members of the class, such as helping a classmate with an assignment, sharing a toy, and so on.

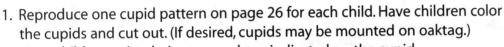

Step 2

MOUSE BEANBAG

You need:
• scissors
• pen or marker
• red felt
• glue
• dried beans
• needle and thread

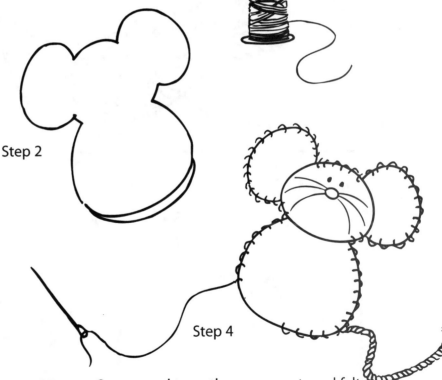

Step 4

1. Reproduce the mouse pattern on page 27 once. Cut out and trace the mouse onto red felt twice for each child in the class.
2. Help children cut out the felt mice. Then help each child place two mice together and glue around the edges, leaving a small opening at the bottom, as shown.
3. Fill each beanbag with dried beans, then finish gluing the edges together.
4. Sew around the edges, as shown, to secure. Let children draw faces on their mice.
5. If desired, use yarn to make tails for the mice.

Cupid Pattern

Mouse Beanbag Pattern

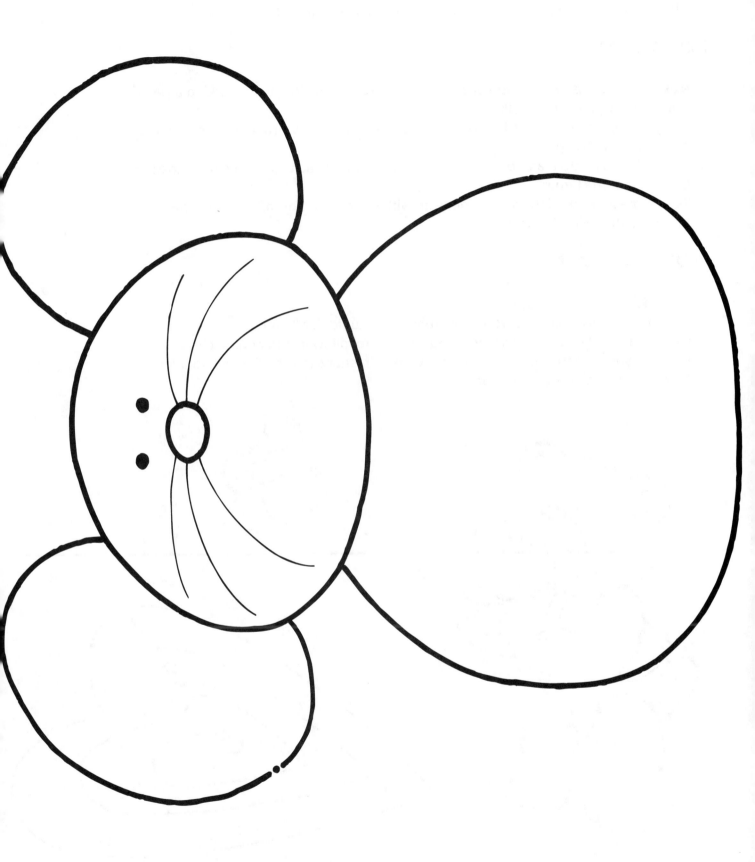

Use the mouse beanbag (see page 25) to play the following games.

BEANBAG TOSS

1. Make a target toss in the shape of concentric hearts on the floor with masking tape or outside on asphalt with chalk.
2. Assign points to each of the hearts. The largest heart may be worth one point and the smallest worth five points.
3. Divide the class into teams of four to six players each. Let each team take turns tossing beanbags at the target.
4. Keep score for each of the teams. The team with the most points after each player has had a turn wins the game.

"CUPID SAYS" GAME

1. Give each child a beanbag.
2. Play the game like "Simon Says" except substitute "Cupid" for "Simon."
3. Help reinforce directional skills by asking children to follow instructions such as "Cupid says, 'Put your beanbag over your head.'" (Other directions may be "behind your knees," "between your elbows," and so on.)

VALENTINE'S DAY LOTTO GAME

HOW TO MAKE

You need:
- crayons or markers
- glue
- oaktag
- scissors
- letter sized-file folder
- envelope

1. Reproduce the game boards on pages 31 and 32 twice. Color each picture on the game boards exactly alike. One set will serve as game boards, the other as game cards.
2. Mount two game boards on 9" x 12" pieces of oaktag.
3. Mount the other two game boards on oaktag and cut apart along the lines.
4. Reproduce the "How to Play" instructions on page 30. Color, cut out, and mount on the outside of a file folder.
5. Store the game boards inside the file folder. Glue an envelope to the back of the folder to store the game cards.

VALENTINE'S DAY LOTTO GAME

HOW TO PLAY
(for 2 to 3 players)

1. Each player chooses one of the lotto game boards on pages 31 and 32 and sits in front of it. Players agree upon what lotto formation they would like to complete on their game boards. For example, players may choose to do the letter *X, L,* or *T,* or do a picture frame square, or cover the entire game board.
2. Place all game cards in a pile.
3. The youngest player goes first. That player draws a card from the pile and places it on the matching picture on his or her game board. Then the next player goes.
4. If a player already has the game card he or she has drawn, the card is placed at the bottom of the pile of game cards and the next player goes.
5. The first player to cover the chosen formation is the winner.

Valentine's Day Lotto Game Patterns

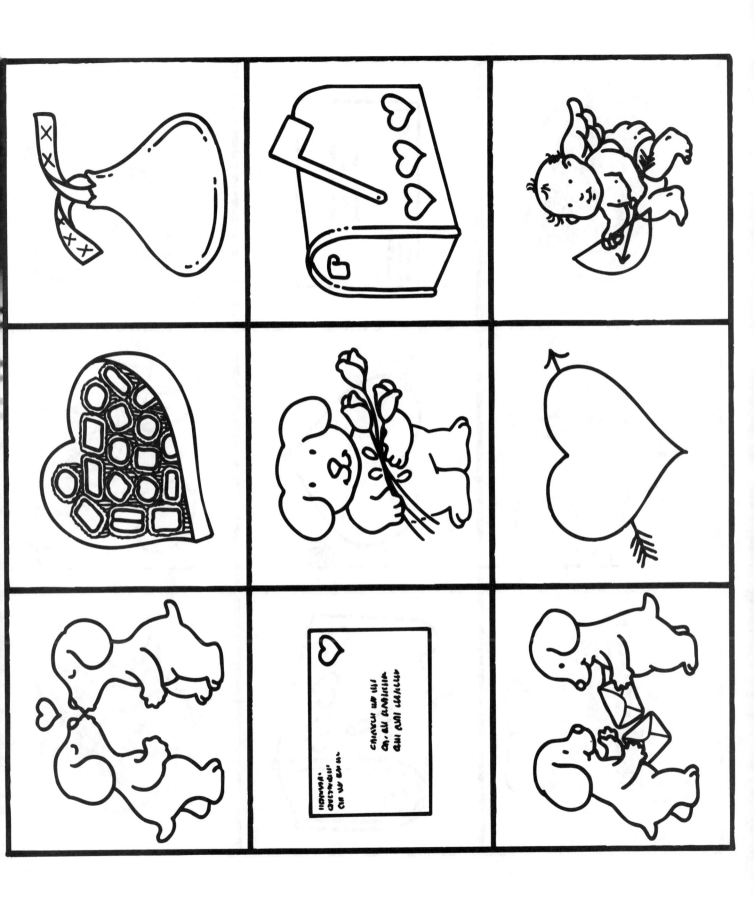

Valentine's Day Lotto Game Patterns

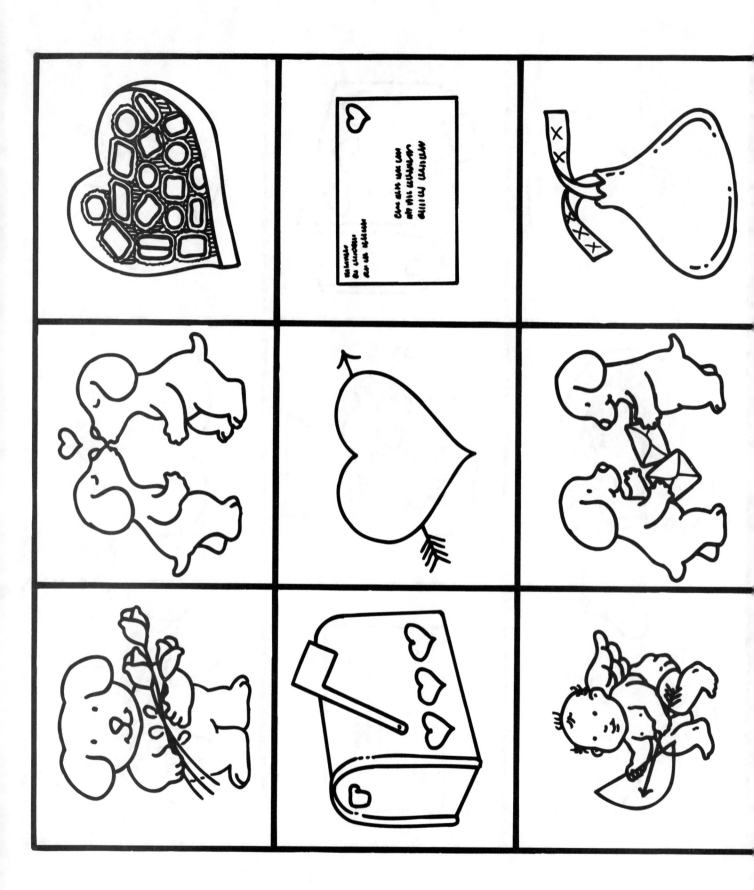

PRESIDENT'S DAY CLASS DISCUSSION

Ask the class if anyone has heard of George Washington or Abraham Lincoln. Tell children that many years ago, George Washington helped our country win its freedom. Since he was such a good leader during this time, people decided that he should continue to be the leader of the country, and so he became our first president. Explain that many people call him the father of our country. Then explain that another president, Abraham Lincoln, helped all the people in our country become free, and he helped keep the United States together during the Civil War, a terrible war that divided the states. Tell children these are some of the reasons why we honor George Washington and Abraham Lincoln.

Ask volunteers to name some of the responsibilities a president has. Make a list of all the jobs, comparing them to actual duties, such as being head of the armed forces, helping to make laws, meeting with leaders from other countries, and choosing people to help run our country.

See if anyone knows the name of our current president. Ask children whether they would like to be president someday. Ask them what changes they would make if they became president.

Encourage children to think of things that have the name "Washington" or "Lincoln." Bring in pictures of the Washington Monument, the Lincoln Memorial, and so on. Show children pennies, quarters, and dollar bills that depict Washington's and Lincoln's likenesses.

PRESIDENT'S DAY MOBILE

You need:
- crayons or markers
- oaktag
- scissors
- hole puncher
- 12" pieces of yarn
- hangers (one per child)

1. Reproduce all the patterns on pages 35 through 37 once for each child. Have children color, mount on oaktag, and cut out.
2. Help children punch holes at the top of each pattern, as shown. Then thread and knot a piece of yarn through each hole.
3. Have children tie the loose ends of the yarn to a hanger, as shown. Space the yarn so that the patterns hang freely with ample room between them.
4. Suspend the hangers from a cord or rod running across the classroom ceiling.

Step 2

Step 3

President's Day Mobile Patterns

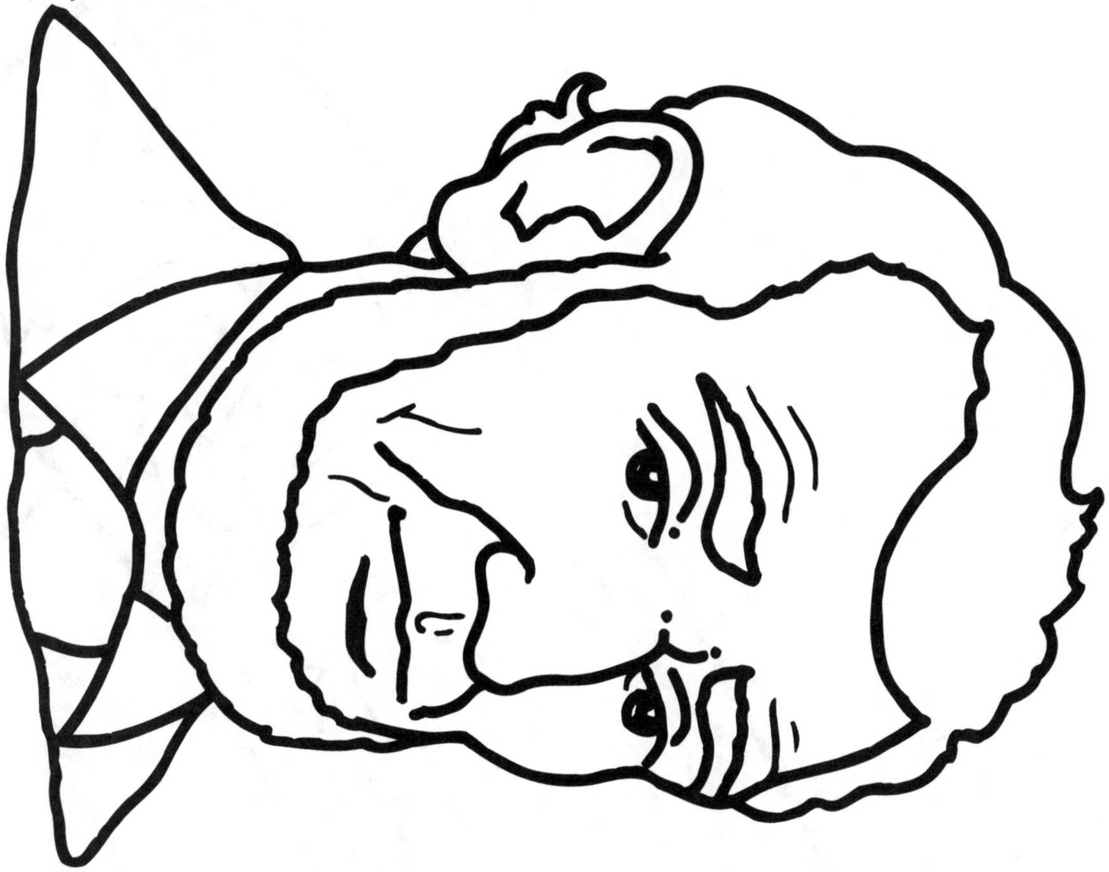

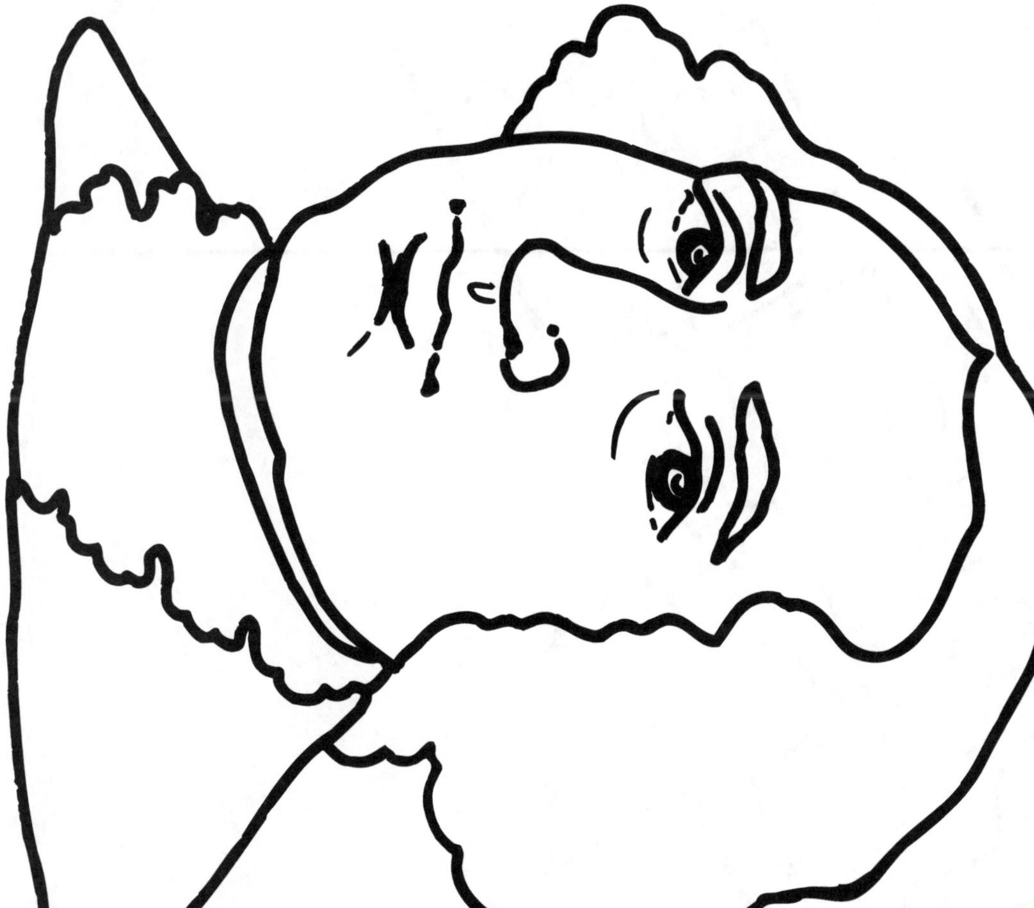

President's Day Mobile Pattern

LEGENDS OF THE PRESIDENTS

You need:
- oaktag
- scissors
- glue
- crayons or markers
- 2" x 24" strips of construction paper
- stapler

There are many famous stories, or legends, about George Washington and Abraham Lincoln. Share the following two legends with the class. Then invite children to prepare a reenactment of each story. Children playing Washington or Lincoln can use the face patterns on page 35 to prepare masks. They can use the patterns on pages 36 and 37 as props as they retell each story.

Washington and the Cherry Tree

As a young boy, George Washington liked to play in the yard outside his home. A cherry tree stood in the yard. One day, George took an axe and cut down the cherry tree.

Later, George's father came home and saw the cherry tree was cut down. He was very upset. He called out, "Who cut down this cherry tree?"

Young George was worried. He knew he had done something wrong. He was afraid he would be punished if he told the truth. But he also knew it was wrong to tell a lie.

Finally, George stood before his father and said, "Father, I cannot tell a lie. I chopped down the cherry tree." George's father was not happy that George had cut down the tree. But he was happy that his son had chosen not to tell a lie.

Lincoln's Love of Learning

As a young boy, Abraham Lincoln lived in a log cabin on the frontier. He loved to read. But there were not many schools, teachers, or books around. Still, young Abe managed to teach himself how to read.

Abe would often walk several miles to the nearest library to get new books to read. Some of his favorite books were *Robinson Crusoe*, *Aesop's Fables*, and a book on United States history. He always made sure to return the books on time, too.

On the frontier, there was not much paper available. Young Abe often did arithmetic problems on wooden boards. He would shave the boards with a knife, and use them over and over. With the little paper he had, Abe even made his own arithmetic book!

PRESIDENT'S DAY BULLETIN BOARD

You need:
• scissors
• black, white, red, and blue construction paper
• stapler
• white chalk
• crayons or markers

1. Reproduce all the patterns on pages 40 through 42 once. Cut them out and trace onto black construction paper.
2. Cut out the figures to make silhouettes, as shown.
3. Cover a bulletin board with white construction paper to make the background for a flag. Using red construction paper, cut seven strips the length of the bulletin board. To determine the width of each strip, divide the width of the base you are using on the bulletin board by 13.
4. Staple one red strip on the bottom and one red strip across the top. Arrange the five remaining red strips to alternate with white spaces that are the same width.
5. Attach a blue construction-paper rectangle in the top left corner. Use white chalk to draw 50 stars on the blue paper.
6. Staple the silhouettes of Washington and Lincoln over the flag. Label the bulletin board "Our America."
7. Give the class some background information about the two presidents. Have children draw pictures of events in Washington's and Lincoln's lives. Attach the pictures to the bulletin board and ask volunteers to explain what their illustrations represent.

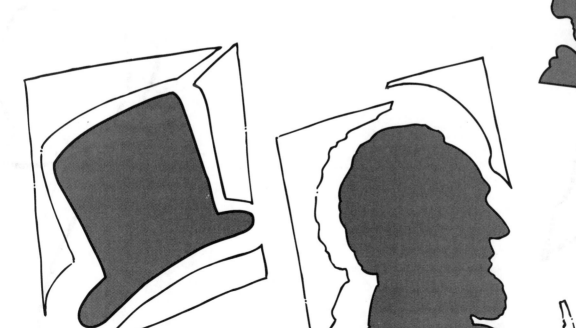

President's Day Bulletin Board Pattern—Lincoln's Hat

WASHINGTON'S THREE-CORNERED HAT

You need:
- 9" x 12" white construction paper
- scissors
- crayons or markers
- stapler
- 6" pieces of white yarn
- string

1. Help each child fold a 9" x 12" piece of white construction paper in thirds lengthwise, as shown.
2. Help children cut along the folds, creating three 3" x 12" strips.
3. Let children use crayons or markers to decorate their hats.
4. Staple the ends of the strips together, as shown, to create a triangular-shaped three-cornered hat.
5. Give each child fifteen 6" pieces of white yarn. Help each child gather the pieces together, then use a piece of string to tie a knot at one end, as shown.
6. Staple the knotted end to one side of the hat. Give each child another piece of yarn to complete the ponytail, as shown.
7. Have children wear their hats with ponytails in back. Explain to children that in George Washington's time, men wore long stockings and pants that came down only to their knees, and women wore long dresses down their ankles. Show the class pictures of such outfits. Tell them that women did not go to school, but instead stayed home and learned to sew and play musical instruments, such as the harpsichord, which looks like a small piano. Explain that people had to make everything they owned: they wove their own cloth, made their own candles, grew or hunted for their own food. Tell children that there was no electricity and there were no cars.
8. Play a record of some harpsichord music written by Bach, who lived around Washington's time. Let children wear their hats as they dance to the harpsichord.

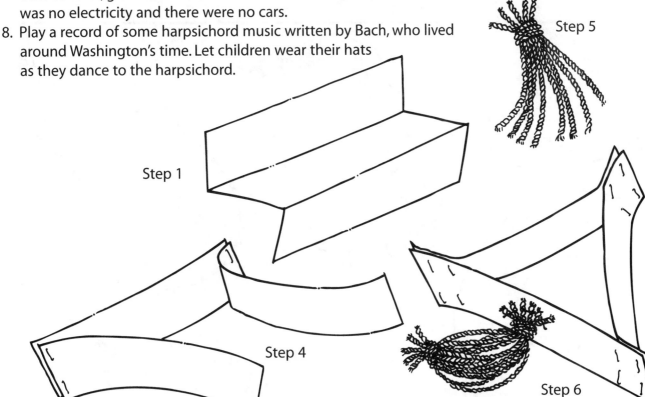

Step 1

Step 5

Step 4

Step 6

LINCOLN'S STOVEPIPE HAT

You need:
• 12" x 18" black construction paper
• scissors
• tape
• hole puncher
• 14" pieces of yarn

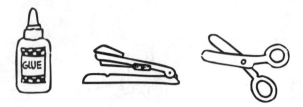

1. Give each child two 12" x 18" pieces of black construction paper. Help children cut around the corners of one piece of paper to create an oval shape, as shown.
2. Help each child cut a 5" circle in the middle of the oval, as shown.
3. Have each child cut a slit every 2" along one of the long sides of the second piece of construction paper to create tabs. Help children roll the papers into cylinder shapes and secure with tape, as shown.
4. Tell children to fold the tabs up. Help children fit the cylinders inside the holes and tape the tabs to the undersides of the hats.
5. Punch holes in the sides of the hats and help children thread 14" pieces of yarn through the holes, as shown. Have children tie the yarn under their chins.
6. While celebrating Lincoln's birthday, let children wear the stovepipe hats as they play with Lincoln Logs or build their own log cabins using craft sticks.

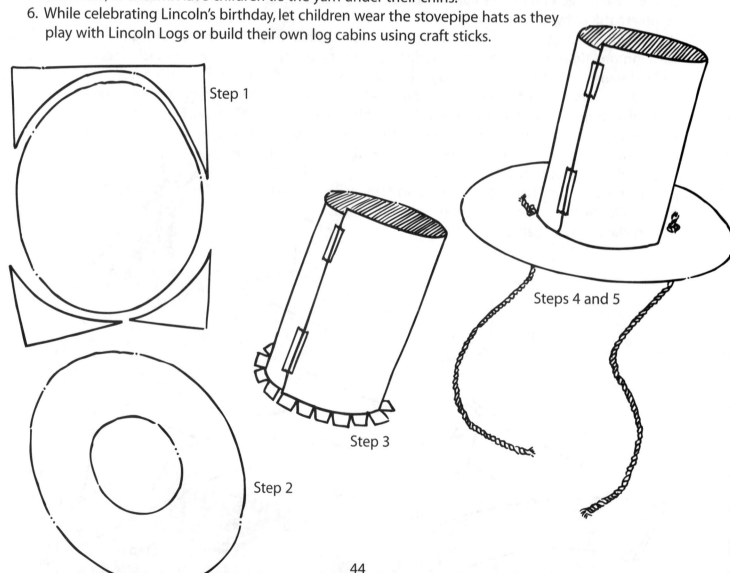

Step 1

Step 2

Step 3

Steps 4 and 5

FRIENDSHIP SONG

To celebrate International Friendship Day, on February 19th, invite children to sing the following song. Have children sit in a circle, with one child standing in the middle. The entire group starts to sing the song below. Just before the last line, the child in the middle points to a classmate in the circle and sings the line alone, inserting the classmate's name. The chosen classmate then steps into the middle and the two hold hands.

The song is sung again by the group. This time, the child who was just chosen sings the last line. He or she points to another "friend," who then steps into the middle and holds hands.

Continue singing until everyone is in the middle, holding hands.

(sung to the tune of "The Farmer in the Dell")

Oh, who will be my friend?
My friend until the end?
A friend to play with any day,
_____ will be my friend!

Literature Connection

FABLES OF FRIENDSHIP FLANNEL BOARD

HOW TO MAKE

You need:
• crayons or markers
• glue
• oaktag
• scissors
• scraps of flannel or sandpaper

1. Reproduce all the flannel board patterns on pages 47 through 49 once.
2. Color the figures and props. Mount on oaktag and cut out.
3. Cut 1" squares of flannel or sandpaper. Glue the squares to the backs of the figures and props, using several scraps for the larger patterns, as shown.
4. Before you read the fables to children, explain to them that a fable is a short story that teaches a lesson. Then, as you read the fables, put the characters on the flannel board and move them at appropriate times during the stories.

Step 3

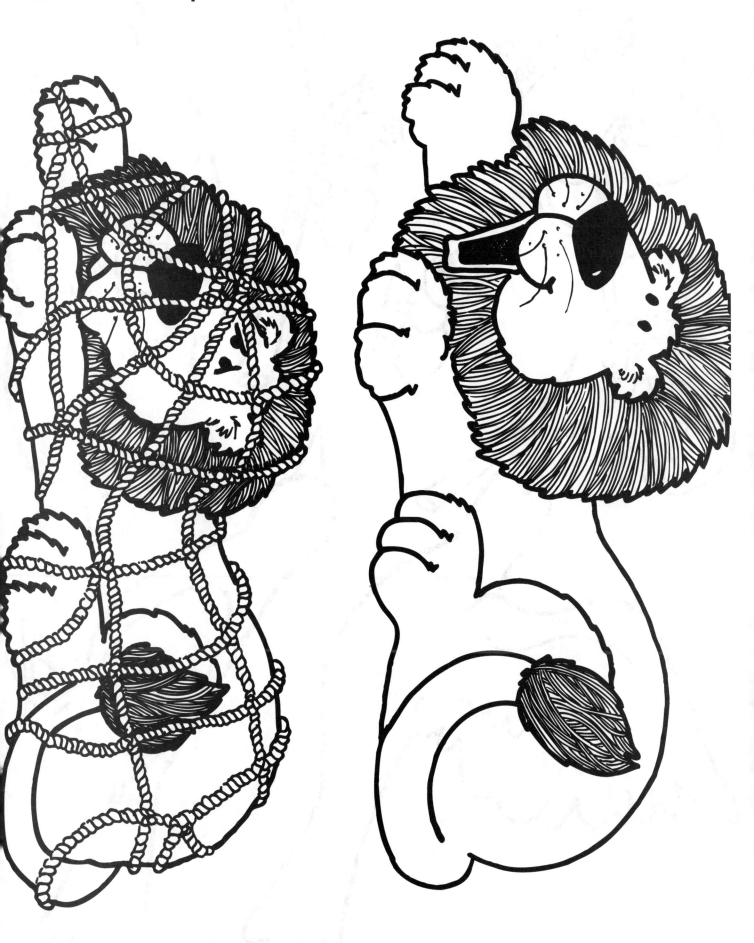

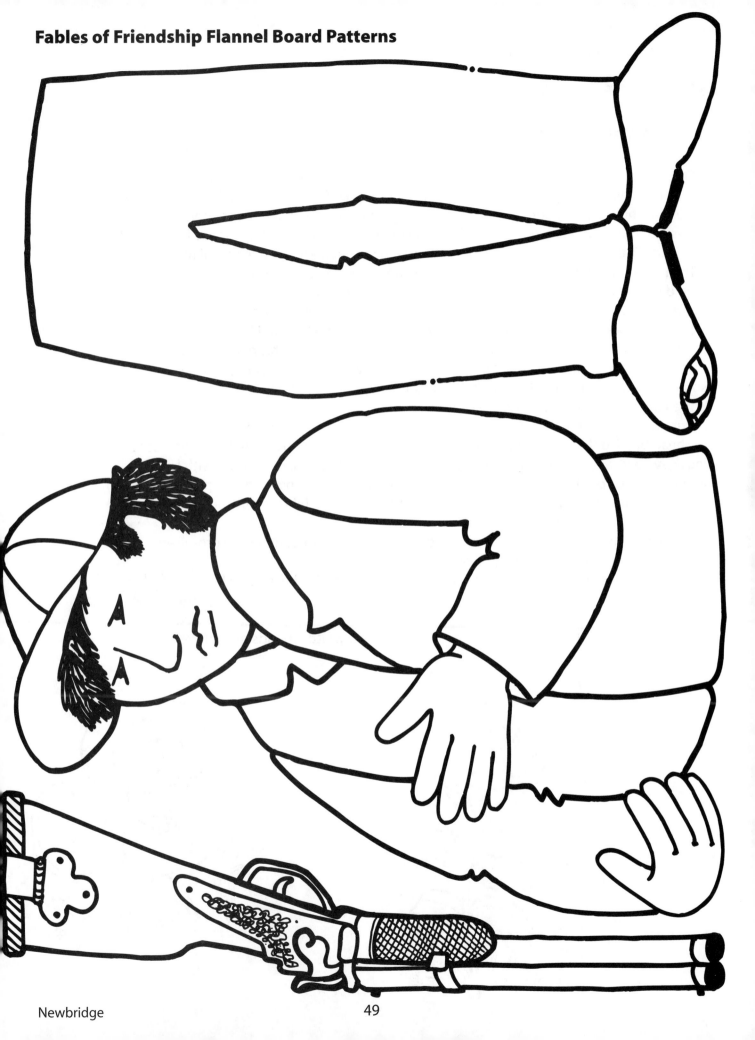

FABLES OF FRIENDSHIP FLANNEL BOARD STORIES

THE LION AND THE MOUSE

One summer day in the forest, a lion, the king of all beasts, was taking a nap. As he snored peacefully, a very small mouse ran over the top of his paw. Still half asleep, the lion lifted his other paw high and brought it down on top of the mouse, catching her between his sharp claws. Her pitiful squeaks woke him fully. As he glanced down at the tiny mouse he yawned and said, "This is hardly a mouthful for me. It would take at least 100 mice to fill me up."

The mouse shivered and shook beneath the lion's paw, pleading for her life. She said, "It would not be worth your time to eat me, King Lion. I hope that you are as kind as you are strong. Let me go, King Lion, and someday you will be thankful you did."

The lion roared loudly with laughter. "Why should I be thankful that I let you go? How could such a tiny creature as you do anything for me?" But the lion lifted his paw, and the mouse was allowed to run free. As she scampered away she said, "Thank you, King Lion. Even someone as small as I may be of help to you someday."

The lion just chuckled and then fell back asleep.

During the fall of that same year, the lion was parading through the forest, holding his head high so that all the animals might see his lovely mane. Suddenly, his magnificent legs gave way and he fell, hopelessly tangled in a net that had been covered with leaves and branches. Poor King Lion roared louder and louder, feeling angry and stupid and even a little scared. When the lion stopped roaring to catch his breath, he heard a little squeak beside his ear.

It was a mouse, the very same mouse whom he had let escape. She said, "I promised to help you someday, King Lion. And now I have my chance."

The little mouse chewed for a time, and King Lion was finally able to crawl out of the net.

The moral of the story is: Kindness is never thrown away. Little friends may prove to be great friends.

THE ANT AND THE DOVE

Once upon a time, a dove was busy building her nest in a tree. She flew this way and that, collecting short twigs and long twigs to weave into the nest. As she swooped down to gather an especially nice twig on a low branch near the ground, she heard a faint splashing noise. An ant had fallen into a rain puddle and was thrashing around. It looked as if the ant were drowning.

Quickly the dove dropped the twig into the puddle. The ant managed to scramble up on the twig, and there he rested, panting, until the twig floated to the edge of the puddle.

The ant looked up to find the dove who had saved him, but she had gone back to building her nest. Then the ant began his journey home, wishing he could do something to let the dove know how grateful he was for her help. He stopped for a moment and listened to some footsteps coming closer and closer. He could see that the footsteps were being made by a man. The steps stopped. The ant watched the man lift something long and heavy over one shoulder. The man closed one eye, taking aim. Looking around, the ant could see the dove building her nest. He knew that the man was aiming at the dove.

The ant rushed toward the man. His shoes were old and worn. One of his toes was sticking out through a hole. The ant moved toward the toe and bit it as hard as he could. With a yelp of surprise, the man jumped and pointed his gun into the air. The gun went off with a loud blast, startling the dove, who flew to safety. And the little ant went home, happy that he was able to help the dove.

The moral of the story is: One good turn deserves another.

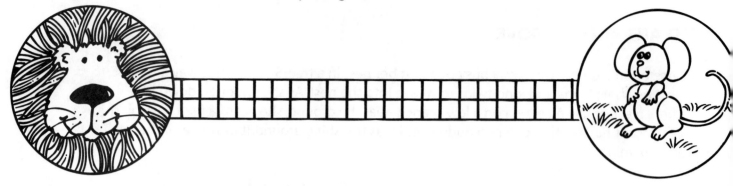

AESOP'S FABLES CLASS DISCUSSION

1. Aesop's fables came originally from the country of Greece, and they have been told by parents and grandparents to children for a long, long time.
2. Tell children that a moral of a story is the lesson you learn from the story. Talk about the morals in each of the fables. Ask volunteers to tell other stories that have a moral.
3. Once children have heard the stories, ask them to think of some ways in which the two stories are alike, and some ways in which they are different.
4. Ask children to imagine that the stories ended differently. What might have happened instead?

DRAMATIZE THE FABLES

Aesop's fables make good stories for children to reenact because they are short, simple, and have few characters.

1. Ask two volunteers to play the parts of the lion and the mouse, using their bodies and short sentences to tell what happened in the story.
2. Ask three volunteers to play the parts of the ant, the dove, and the hunter and act out the story of the ant and the dove.
3. Have children retell the story of the lion and the mouse, and the story of the ant and the dove, on the flannel board, using the flannel board characters.
4. Then ask volunteers to change the endings of the fables, using the flannel board characters and the ideas from the Aesop's Fables Class Discussion.
5. During free time, allow children to make up new stories using the flannel board characters.

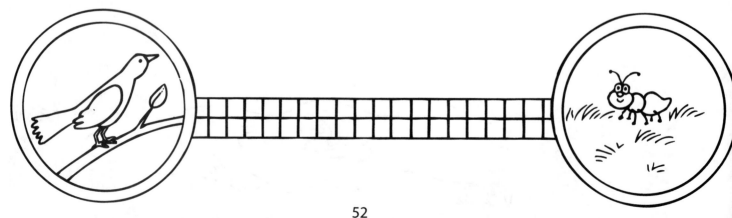

ANIMAL FAMILIES

The lion and the mouse are both furry animals with four legs and a tail. The dove has feathers and wings. The ant is an insect with six legs. Cut out the pictures of the animals below. Glue them under the pictures of the animals that have the same features.

Newbridge

53

FRIENDSHIP DAY RECOMMENDED READING

Read some of the following books to the class. Place the books on a reading table or in a bookcase so that children may look at them during free time.

Best Friends by Steven Kellogg, published by Dial.
Clifford's Family by Norman Bridwell, published by Scholastic.
Do You Want to Be My Friend? By Eric Carle, published by Crowell.
Frog and Toad Are Friends by Arnold Lobel, published by HarperCollins.
A Letter to Amy by Ezra Jack Keats, published by HarperCollins.
May I Bring a Friend? by Beatrice Schenk de Regniers, published by Atheneum.
Our Animal Friends at Maple Hill Farm by Alice and Martin Provensen, published by Random House.
Will I Have a Friend? by Miriam Cohen, published by Macmillan.

HEALTHY TEETH FILE-FOLDER GAME

HOW TO MAKE

You need:
- crayons or markers
- glue
- clear contact paper
- scissors
- stapler
- oaktag
- letter-sized file folder

1. Reproduce the game board on pages 58 and 59 and "How to Play" instructions on page 56 once. Reproduce all game cards on page 57 one time for each group.
2. Have children color the game board and the game cards. Then mount the cards on oaktag and cut out.
3. Have each child find a small item to use for a playing piece (eraser, paper clip, safety pin, etc.) or use markers from a previous game.
4. Glue the game board to the inside of a letter-sized file folder.
5. Glue the "How to Play" instructions to the front of the folder and laminate.

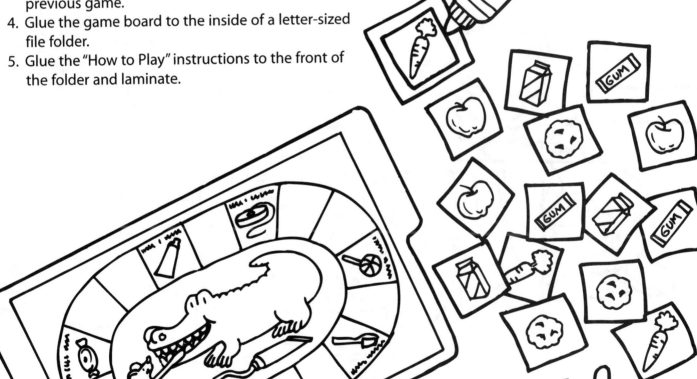

HEALTHY TEETH FILE-FOLDER GAME

HOW TO PLAY
(for 2 to 4 players)

1. All game cards are shuffled and placed facedown in a pile in the middle of the board. All playing pieces are placed on the space on the board marked "Start."
2. Players go in alphabetical order by first name. The first player draws a card and shows it to the other players. The player decides whether the picture on the card is "good" or "bad" for their teeth. As long as the player answers correctly, he/she then moves ahead one space. If the player answers incorrectly, he/she loses a turn.
3. The other players follow the same procedure. If a player lands on a special space, he/she must follow the instructions shown.
4. The first player to go around the entire board and land on the space marked "Finish" wins the game.

Healthy Teeth File-Folder Game Card Patterns

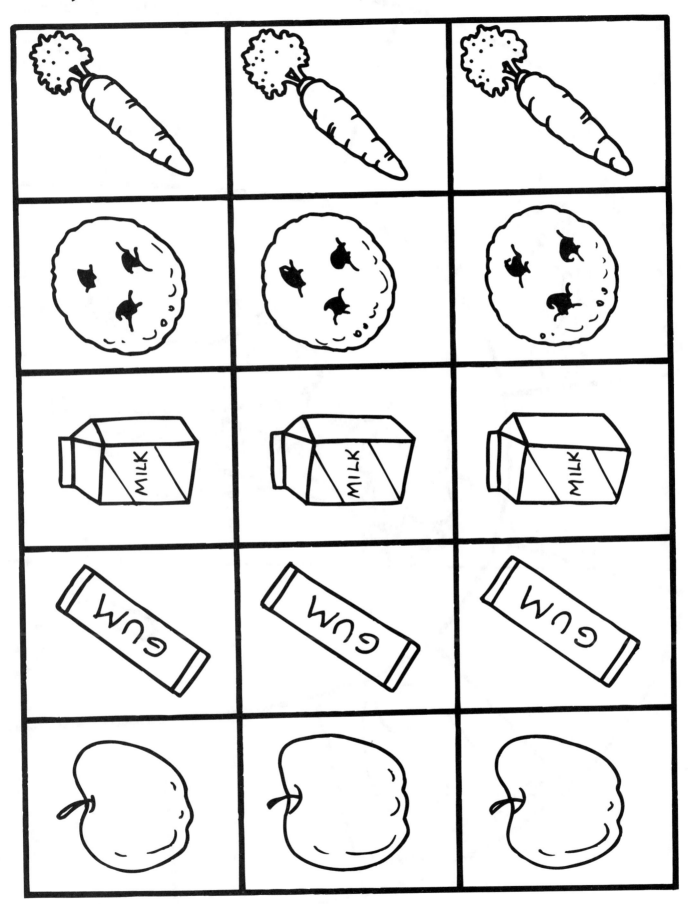

MOVE 3 SPACES

TOOTHPASTE

DO NOT MOVE

MOVE 2 SPACES

START

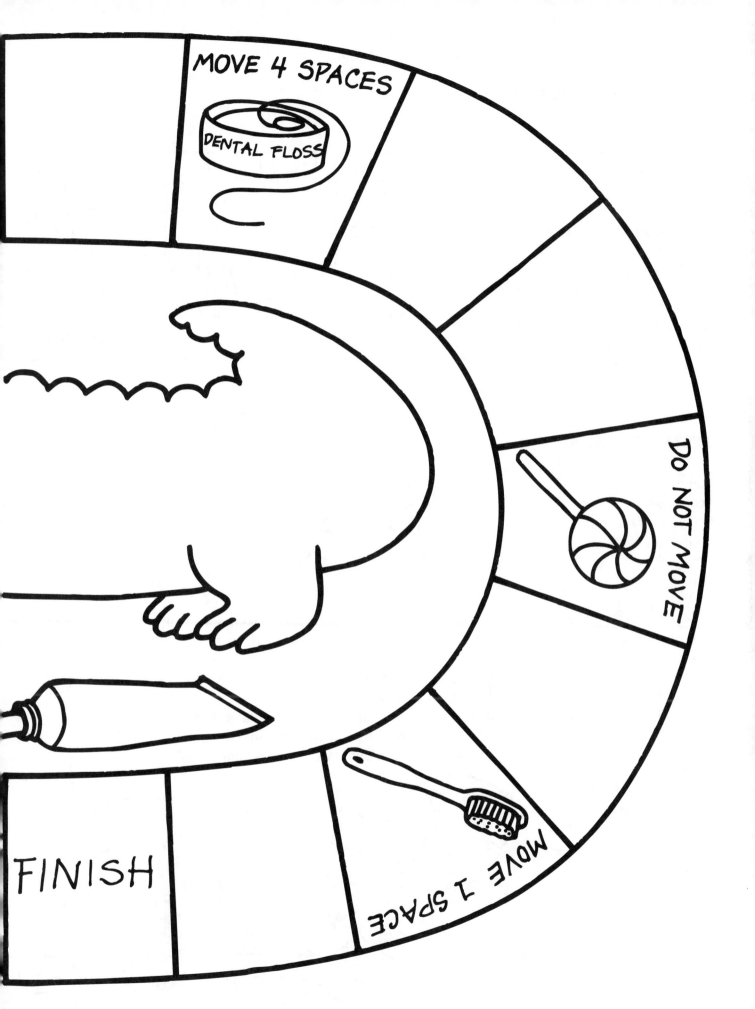

MOVE 4 SPACES

DENTAL FLOSS

Do NOT MOVE

MOVE 1 SPACE

FINISH

HEALTHY TEETH POSTERS

You need:
• crayons or markers
• oaktag
• glue

After children learn about teeth and oral hygiene, have them work individually or with partners to create posters that promote good tooth care. Children can make up their own slogans or copy one of these to write on their poster, along with original artwork.

TEETH COLLAGES

You need:
• construction paper
• crayons or markers
• scissors
• magazines
• glue

1. Reproduce the game cards several times. Let each child choose to do either a "healthy" teeth collage or an "unhealthy" teeth collage. Give each child the cards that go with his/her collage.
2. Give each child one piece of construction paper. Have children paste down the game cards first and write an appropriate title on their collage.
3. Then have them look through old magazines and cut out anything related to their game cards. For example, if a child chose the "healthy" collage, pictures of vegetables, fruits, or milk products would be good ones to cut out. Have children glue all their cutouts onto the construction paper.
4. Hang the collages around the room to remind the children of healthy foods they should eat to keep healthy teeth.

HEALTHY TEETH MOBILE

You need:
• crayons or markers
• scissors
• hole puncher
• yarn
• hanger

1. Reproduce the tooth fairy, toothbrush, toothpaste, and dental floss patterns on pages 62 and 64 once for each child. Reproduce the tooth pattern on page 63 twice for each child. Have children color and cut out.
2. Punch holes in the toothbrush, toothpaste, and tooth figures.
3. Give each child five pieces of yarn, varying in length from 8" to 12". Help children thread the pieces of yarn through the holes and tie knots, as shown.
4. Give each child a hanger. Help each child tie the five healthy tooth figures across the length of the hanger, as shown. Tape each knot to the hanger to keep the figures in place.
5. Have children tape the tooth fairy across the top of the hanger, as shown.
6. Ask children to tie a long piece of yarn to the top of the hanger to complete the mobile. Display the mobiles around the classroom during February, which is Dental Health Month. At the end of the month, let children take the mobiles home to remind them of the importance of good dental care.

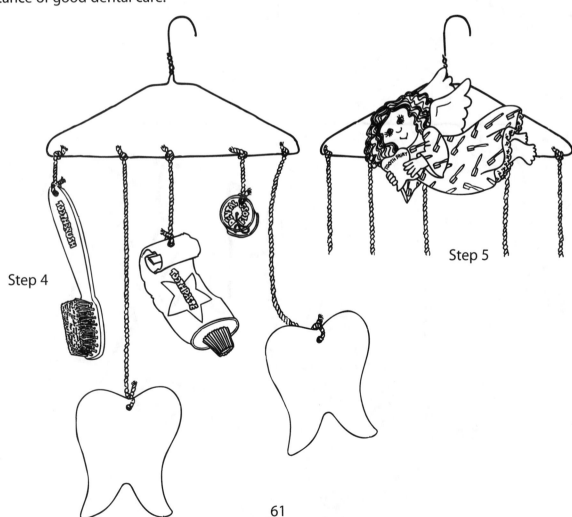

Step 4

Step 5

Healthy Teeth Mobile Pattern

TOOTH FAIRY

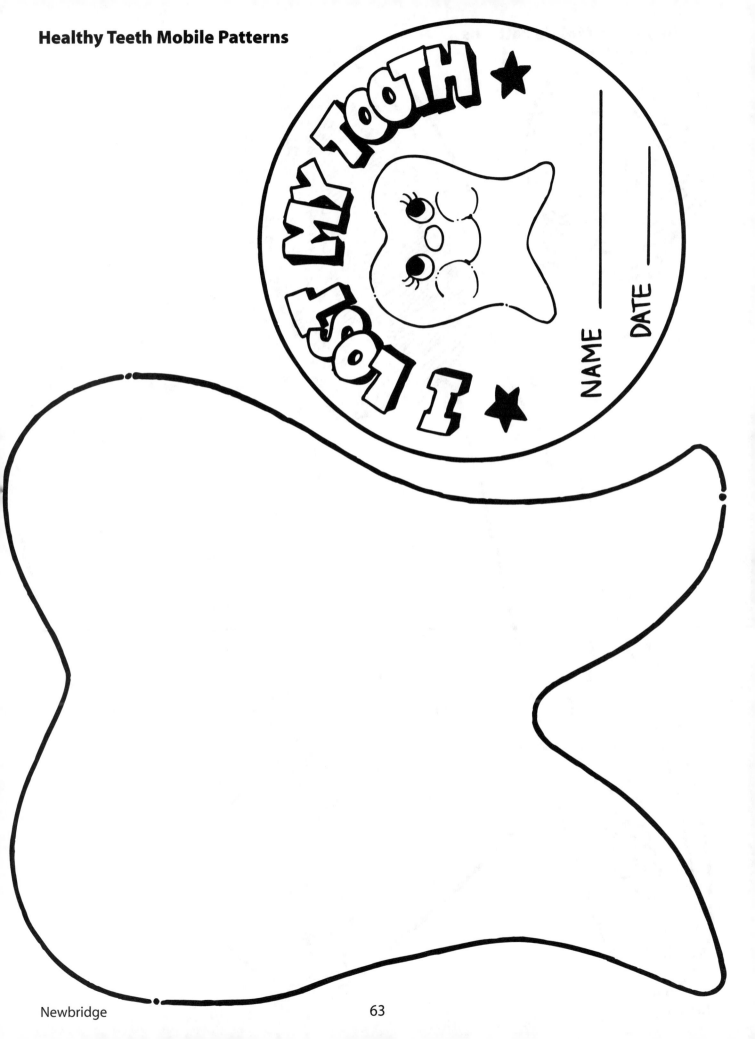

I LOST MY TOOTH ★

★

NAME _____

DATE _____

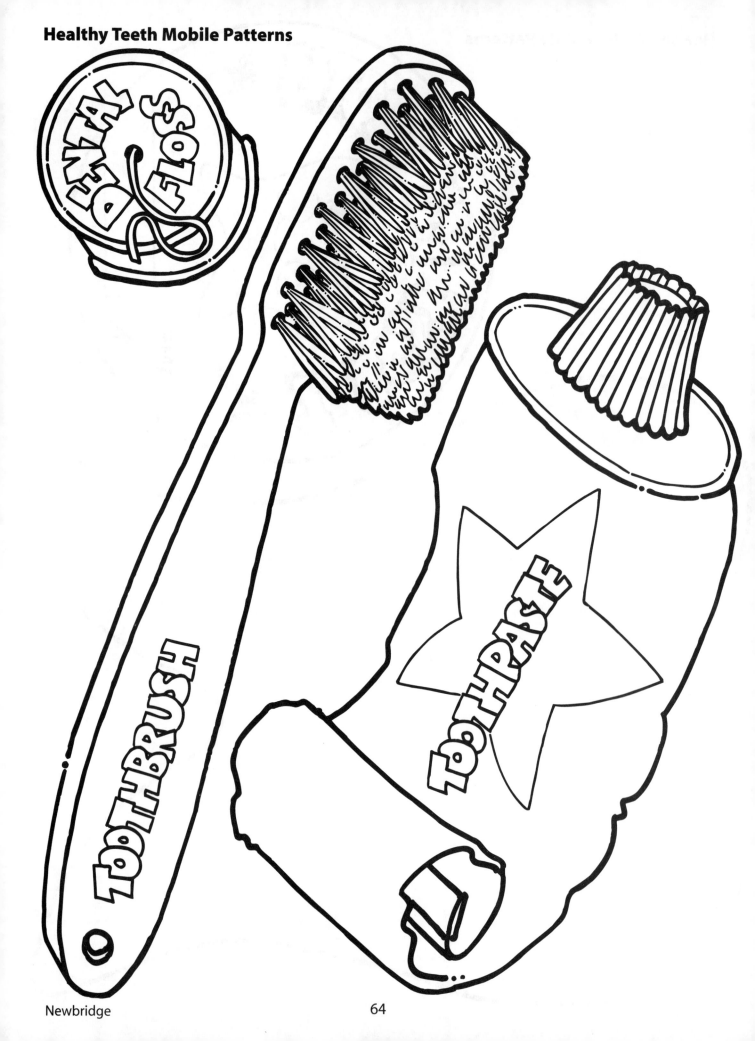

HAPPY TOOTH, SAD TOOTH BOOK

You need:
- scissors
- colored construction paper
- glue
- hole puncher
- yarn
- crayons or markers
- old magazines

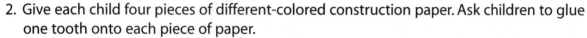

1. Reproduce the tooth pattern on page 63 four times for each child and cut out.
2. Give each child four pieces of different-colored construction paper. Ask children to glue one tooth onto each piece of paper.
3. Have children place the pieces of paper on top of one another to make a book. Punch holes in the upper left and lower left corners of each book, and help children thread yarn through the holes and tie knots.
4. On the front cover, have children write "Happy Tooth, Sad Tooth Book" or "My Tooth Book," and then decorate.
5. Have each child draw a happy face on the second page of the book. Ask children to find pictures in old magazines of healthy foods that are good for teeth, such as fruit, vegetables, milk, and so on.
6. Have each child cut out and glue the pictures of healthy foods onto the Happy Tooth page.

7. On the third page of the book, ask each child to draw a sad face, and then find pictures of unhealthy foods (like soda, candy, and so on). Ask children to cut out these pictures and glue them onto the Sad Tooth page.
8. On the last page of their books, have children write or dictate rules for happy teeth.(Younger children may illustrate the rules instead of writing them down.) Rules may also be copied from a group list.

LOSE-A-TOOTH EXPERIENCE CHART

You need:
- crayons or markers
- glue
- oaktag
- scissors
- pushpins or tacks

1. Reproduce the tooth fairy pattern on page 62 once. Color, mount on oaktag, and cut out.
2. Attach the tooth fairy to a wall or bulletin board next to a large sheet of oaktag.
3. Have a class discussion about losing teeth. Ask if anyone in the class has ever had a visit from the tooth fairy. Make an experience chart by asking children who have already lost their first tooth to share their experiences with the rest of the class, such as how and when the tooth fell out.
4. Reproduce two tooth badges on page 63 whenever a child loses a tooth. Give one badge to a child to wear and take home, and place the other badge next to the experience chart. Write the child's name and the date the tooth fell out on the badge.
5. Ask that child to draw a picture of his or her face with the missing tooth.
6. Attach the pictures to the wall or bulletin board next to the tooth fairy.

I LOST MY FIRST TOOTH WHEN I ATE AN APPLE.
JOEY

I RAN INTO A DOOR AND LOST MY TOOTH.
CHRIS

FAMOUS AFRICAN-AMERICANS BULLETIN BOARD

You need:
- crayons or markers
- scissors
- tape
- pushpins or tacks
- Optional: construction paper, stapler

Step 2

1. During Black History Month (February), reproduce all the Famous African-American figures and their biographies on pages 68 through 75 and 77 through 80 once. Color the figures and cut out.
2. Tape together the top and bottom of each figure. Then tape the item that belongs in each figure's hand, as shown.
3. Display the figures on the bulletin board. Attach each story beneath its corresponding figure.
4. If you wish, reproduce all the Famous African-American figures and biographies once for each child. Have children color, cut out, and mount on construction paper. Children may staple their pages together to make a "Famous African-Americans Book" to take home.

JACKIE ROBINSON

As a child, Jackie Robinson was good at many sports, including football, basketball, and running. But his favorite sport was baseball. He could play almost any position well. In college, Jackie played second base on his school's baseball team. People knew that he was good enough to play big-league baseball. But there was a serious problem.

In Jackie's day, black baseball players were not allowed to play on white teams. White players joined the National or American League. But black players joined the Negro National League. Many Americans, both white and black, felt that having separate baseball teams for the races was very unfair. They began demanding that black players be allowed to play in the white leagues. The owner of one white team, the Brooklyn Dodgers, agreed. He searched for a special individual who not only played well, but who could also take the pressure of being professional baseball's first black player. The person he chose was Jackie Robinson.

Jackie knew that playing for the Dodgers would not be easy. Many fans were unhappy about him being on the team. They booed him on the field and called him names. But Jackie didn't yell back. Instead, he showed what an excellent player he was. In 1947, he was voted Rookie of the Year. In 1949, he led the league in stolen bases and was named Most Valuable Player. Jackie helped his team win many championships. In time, even Jackie's enemies came to love him. And his success led the way for more black players to join other teams.

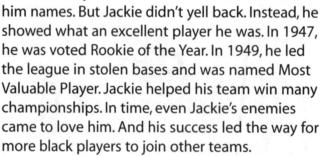

But Jackie did not stop there. After a long career in baseball, he went into business as head of a company. He spoke out for civil rights, and once led 10,000 students in a freedom march in Washington, D.C. Jackie Robinson proved that he was a hero, both on and off the field.

Jackie Robinson Patterns

THURGOOD MARSHALL

Thurgood Marshall made history in 1967, when he became the first African-American to serve on the United States Supreme Court. The Supreme Court is the highest court in our land. That means that its decisions are final. No one can change them. To be a judge on the Supreme Court is a great honor. But for Thurgood Marshall, being the first African-American judge on the court was an even greater honor.

Thurgood was chosen for the Supreme Court because he understood the law well. He was also a fair and honest person. Before becoming a judge, Thurgood worked as a lawyer. He took on many civil rights cases. He defended African-Americans who were not being treated fairly. Thurgood knew all about unfair treatment. His great-grandfather had been a slave. And when Thurgood first applied to law school, he was turned away simply because he was black.

Thurgood worked on his most important case in 1954. At that time, black children were not allowed to go to the same schools as white children. A black parent in Kansas wanted his daughter to attend a white school near their home. He asked Thurgood to argue his case in court. Thurgood gave some very good arguments and won the case. After that, schools were not allowed to be separated by race. And Thurgood Marshall became very famous.

After winning more important cases as a lawyer, Thurgood became a judge. On the Supreme Court, he was known as a very fair individual. He saw to it that African-Americans and other minorities were given the same rights other people had. He even made sure that people arrested for a crime received fair treatment before their trial. Today, Thurgood Marshall is remembered as an outstanding man who fought for the liberty of all Americans.

Thurgood Marshall Patterns

MARIAN ANDERSON

Almost from the time she was born, Marian Anderson loved to sing. As a young girl in Philadelphia, she was part of her church choir. She loved to perform gospel songs and spirituals. People immediately recognized Marian's special talent, and they encouraged her to make singing her career. Being poor, Marian could not always afford to pay for voice lessons. Her church helped pay for some of them. But her singing was so good, her music teacher finally agreed to give her a whole year's worth of lessons free.

At the age of 23, Marian gave her first professional concert, in New York City. Unfortunately, not everyone thought it was a good one. Marian was so upset, she thought of giving up singing altogether. But then she sang again at a special dinner. This time the audience was very happy, and Marian's career was back on track.

Because Marian was black, she faced many serious challenges as a performer. At the time, black people were not allowed to enter certain places. Once she was not even let into a hall where people were waiting just to hear her sing. People across the country were very upset, including Eleanor Roosevelt, the wife of the President. She invited Marian to give another concert four years later in front of the Lincoln Memorial—75,000 people came to listen.

Marian liked to sing many kinds of music, including opera. She traveled around the world giving concerts. In some places, her audiences were small, because people there were not interested in African-American singers. But in many more places, her concerts were sold out. Marian received many honors and medals. She sang for presidents, kings, and queens.

In 1955, Marian became the first African-American to perform a major role at the Metropolitan Opera, in New York City. She was known as a courageous and talented woman who succeeded in a field where no African-Americans had been allowed to succeed before.

Marian Anderson Patterns

GEORGE WASHINGTON CARVER

George Washington Carver was born many years ago as the son of a slave. His mother disappeared when he was just a baby, and George and his brother were raised by another family.

George helped the family by tending to the garden. He loved to grow things. As George grew older, he found that he also loved going to school. George's love of learning caused him to travel to many towns, always looking for bigger and better schools.

Finally, George Washington Carver decided to go to college. It was very unusual for a black man to go to college, but George worked so hard and was so smart that the college asked him to stay and become a teacher of science. But George had already decided to move to Alabama, where many poor farmers lived. He thought he could use his skills as a scientist to help his people.

George showed the farmers in Alabama how to grow better crops. When he told them to grow peanuts, they were surprised. Everyone thought they were hardly better than weeds, but George proved that peanuts were a delicious and healthy food. Because of George Washington Carver, we enjoy peanut butter and other peanut food products today. Think of this famous scientist next time you eat a peanut-butter-and-jelly sandwich!

George Washington Carver

PLANT A PEANUT

You need:
• raw (unroasted) peanuts in the shell
• plastic cups
• potting soil

1. Have children take the peanuts out of the shell. Explain that the inside part of the peanut plant that we eat is actually the seed for a new plant to grow.
2. Give each child a plastic cup filled halfway with potting soil.
3. Tell children to bury their peanuts in soil.
4. Place the cups in a window with plenty of sun. Tell children to keep the soil moist by watering it every two or three days. (Also remind children that too much water is not good for a plant and may kill it.)
5. Let children take their cups home after small plants have sprouted.

PEANUT BUTTER

After reading the biography of George Washington Carver, make the following recipe with your class for everyone to enjoy.

You need:
• 2 lbs. peanuts roasted in the shell
• blender or food processor
• 1/4 cup of vegetable oil
• crackers, bread, celery, or apple slices
Optional: salt

1. Have children take the peanuts out of the shell and remove skins.
2. Put the peanuts in the blender or food processor and grind, adding the vegetable oil a little at a time. (Add salt if desired.) Stop the blender or food processor periodically to show children how the mixture is slowly turning into peanut butter. Two pounds of peanuts should yield about 1 cup of peanut butter.
3. Spread the peanut butter on crackers, bread, celery, or apple slices.

MARTIN LUTHER KING, JR.

Martin Luther King, Jr. grew up in the South as a free man. But when he was very young, he realized that black people like him did not have the same sort of life as white people did. Black people could not go to the same schools as white people. Black people were not allowed to eat in the same restaurants where white people ate. They could not even sit where they wanted on a city bus—all black people had to sit in the back of the bus.

These things made Martin Luther King, Jr. very sad. As he grew up, Martin knew these things needed to change, and he wondered if he could do anything to help.

Martin became a minister. He spoke to many, many people about the things that had made him so sad as a young boy. Many people agreed with Reverend King. Some people were very angry about the way black people were treated in America. But Reverend King showed the people that they could make changes happen without shouting, without guns, and without hurting others. Reverend King led thousands of people, both black and white, to march in Washington, D.C., where the President lives. All the people who marched wanted the same thing: for all people in America to be treated equally.

Slowly, laws began to change. Black and white people began to go to school together. Black and white people ate, worked, and lived next to each other. But not everyone in America was happy. A few people were angry at Reverend King for making all these changes. One day Martin Luther King, Jr. was shot and killed.

People have not forgotten Reverend King's dream of equal rights for all Americans, and they have not forgotten how he brought about changes in a peaceful way. On January 15, Americans celebrate Martin Luther King, Jr.'s birthday. It is a holiday to honor a man and his dreams.

Martin Luther King, Jr. believed all problems should be solved peacefully. Describe some good ways and bad ways to solve problems.

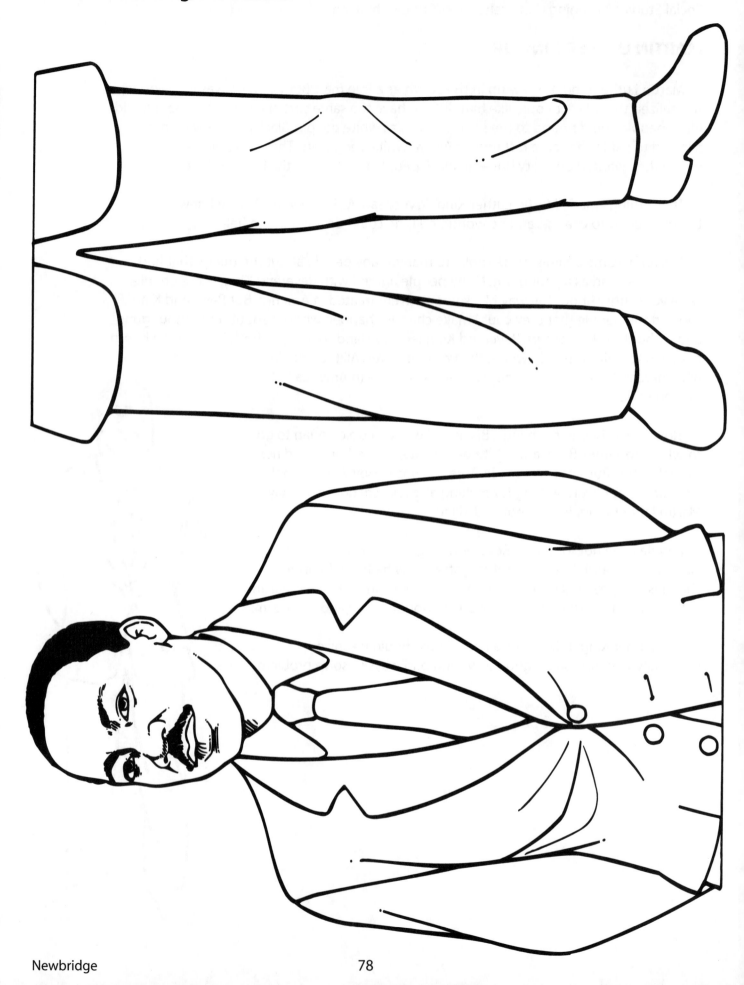

HARRIET TUBMAN

Harriet Tubman was born a slave many years ago. As a young woman, she had to work in the fields all day. Sometimes she worked inside the house, cleaning and taking care of babies. If Harriet did something wrong, or if she didn't work fast enough, she would be beaten by the people who owned her. How she hated being a slave! Harriet grew older and worked harder. She wanted to escape to the North, where she would not have to be a slave any longer. But she was afraid that she would be caught and that her life would be worse than ever.

Finally, late one night, she walked quietly out of her cabin and through the woods. She found a house where she could be safe. The people who owned the house hid her during the day. Then, when it was dark again, they gave her directions to another house where she would be safe. Harriet traveled this way for many nights and hid during many days until she finally reached the North.

The path to freedom for Harriet Tubman was called the Underground Railroad. This was not a real railroad with trains, and it wasn't underground. Instead, the Underground Railroad was a series of houses that black people could go to on their way to the North. It was kept a secret from the people who did not want slavery to end. The Underground Railroad stations were the "safe" houses where people could hide and rest until night came and they could go farther.

Harriet was so grateful for the help she got during her escape to freedom that she decided to go back to the South and help other slaves escape. She made many dangerous trips trying to help others reach freedom. She is remembered as a strong woman of great courage who helped many people become free.